The Zinoviev Controversy
Resolved

The
Zinoviev Controversy Resolved

John Symons

SHEPHEARD-WALWYN (PUBLISHERS) LTD

First published in 2019 by
Shepheard-Walwyn (Publishers) Ltd
107 Parkway House, Sheen Lane,
London SW14 8LS
www.shepheard-walwyn.co.uk
www.ethicaleconomics.org.uk

British Library Cataloguing in Publication Data
A catalogue record of this book
is available from the British Library

ISBN: 978-0-85683-530-8

Typeset by Alacrity, Chesterfield, Sandford, Somerset
Printed and bound in the United Kingdom
by 4edge Limited

In memory of Judy,
my dearly loved
and much loving wife
who helped me so much
with this book
in her last year

Acknowledgements

Judy and I are grateful to Anthony Werner of Shepheard-Walwyn for publishing my books and for all his kindness, skill and wisdom; along with his colleagues Jean Maughan, Andrew Candy, and Catherine Hodgkinson. We are similarly grateful to our friend of forty years, Caroline Standing, for several discussions I have had with her about Zinoviev's letter and about this book since I made the discovery reported here in June 2018.

Contents

1
This Book

THIS SHORT BOOK turns on its head the history of the Zinoviev letter of October 1924 and of all that year's melancholy legacy.

It shows that Grigory Zinoviev, chairman of the Soviet-controlled Comintern and a member with Trotsky and Stalin of the Bolshevik Politburo of the Soviet Union, wrote the letter to the British Communist Party, telling them to manipulate the Labour Party, which was hostile to Communist aims, so as to move the Labour Party to a revolutionary position.

It shows that Zinoviev's letter was not a fabrication by White Russians or by British elements hostile to Mr MacDonald's Labour

Government, as has been widely believed for almost a hundred years.

This is a work of history, and the facts are here for all to see. It also offers, by revealing the truth, healing for the wounds caused by those events in our country's life, a way to put to rest a national tragedy after a century.

2

Introduction

IN HIS INTRODUCTION to a translation of the Greek text of Athanasius' *On the Incarnation*, C.S. Lewis wrote to encourage all students and would-be scholars to read original books and documents rather than commentaries on them.[1]

Unhappily, this vital piece of advice cannot be followed in the case of Zinoviev's letter of the autumn of 1924 because the original has disappeared. Its disappearance is, indeed, one of the mysteries that all inquirers about it have had to tackle. All that we can read is an alleged copy of the letter, in English, set out in chapter

---

1 The essay has happily been reprinted many times, under the title *On the Reading of Old Books*.

three, and a copy of the alleged original, in Russian. The authenticity of both is disputed.

With her Foreign and Commonwealth Office Report[2] and her magisterial book on the Zinoviev Letter,[3] Gill Bennett, one time Chief Historian at the F.C.O., knows more than anyone in the West still alive about this 'mysterious business'. Perhaps only a fool would venture onto her territory, but I hope here to add something new and of interest. In doing so, I express my profound respect for her, especially as I give reasons for rejecting her fundamental conclusion.

I hope to show that an 'old book', never referred to in discussion of the letter, as far as I know, is the key to its understanding and unlocks the mystery.

2 The Report was published in February 1999, under the title, *A most extraordinary and mysterious business: The Zinoviev Letter of 1924.*

3 *The Zinoviev Letter: The Conspiracy that Never Dies*, Oxford University Press, 2018.

3
The Letter

THIS CHAPTER sets out the English text of Zinoviev's letter as it was received in London by the headquarters of the British Secret Intelligence Service, S.I.S., also known as M.I.6, on the 8th of October 1924. It had been sent from the S.I.S. office in Latvia on the 2nd of October. S.I.S. also received a text of the letter in Russian on the 12th of December, marked (in Russian) 'Copy' in its top right hand corner.

The text of the English letter given here includes insertions at the relevant points of this author's translations of the Russian text where its meaning differs, even slightly, from the English: these translations are indicated by these [square brackets].

The phrasing of the English document in places strongly suggests both that this document was a translation rather than an original and that the translation of the original Russian text, whether an authentic letter from the Comintern or not, was made by a person whose first language was not English. Indeed, the English text is so stilted that it is very unlikely to have been written by a native English-speaker and it reads like an imperfect translation made by a Russian.

The mistake referred to in note 5 below is important and striking. It seems to exclude the possibility that the original of the letter was a forgery in English which was later translated into Russian only when its authenticity was questioned systematically in British official circles in November 1924. The Russian text at the point marked by note 5 is more compromising than is the English, dealing as it does with the manipulation of the Labour Party by the Communists, and a forger would have grasped that. If we are dealing with a forgery, the forgery is probably the Russian text later translated into English. Besides, no native English speaker would have written 'SSSR' rather than 'USSR', see note 4.

Instructions to the British Communist Party

Executive Committee,   VERY SECRET
Third
Communist International.

Praesidium.

                To the Central Committee
Sept 15th 1924.   British Communist Party.

Moscow.

Dear Comrades,

The time is approaching for the Parliament of England to consider [to scrutinise] the Treaty concluded between the Governments of Great Britain and the S[4]SSR for the purpose of

4 This 'S' stands for 'Soyuz', the Russian for 'Union'.

ratification. The fierce campaign raised by the British bourgeoisie around the question shows that the majority of the same, together with reactionary circles, are against [are moving against] the Treaty for the purpose of breaking off an agreement consolidating the ties between the proletariats [proletariat] of the two countries [and] leading to the restoration [establishment] of normal relations between England and the SSSR.

The proletariat of Great Britain, which pronounced its weighty word when danger threatened of a break-off of the past negotiations, and compelled the Government of MacDonald to conclude the Treaty, must show the greatest possible energy in the further struggle for ratification [of the treaty] and against the endeavours of British capitalists to compel Parliament to annul it [the agreement].

It is indispensable to stir up the [inert] masses of the British proletariat, to bring into movement the army of unemployed proletarians, whose position can be improved only after a loan has been granted to the SSSR for the restoration of her economies [economic life] and when business collaboration between the British and Russian proletariats [proletariat] has been put in order. It is imperative that the group in the Labour Party sympathising with the Treaty should bring increased pressure to bear upon the Government and parliamentary circles in favour of the ratification of the Treaty. [It is imperative to bring a forceful influence in favour of the ratification of the Treaty on the Government, Parliamentary circles, by means of the left-wing group in the Labour Party which sympathises with the Treaty.][5]

Keep close observation over the leaders of the Labour Party, because those [they] may easily be found in the leading strings[6] of the bourgeoisie [turn out to be under the thumb of the bourgeoisie]. The foreign policy of the Labour Party [government] as it is already represents an inferior copy of the policy of the Curzon Government.[7]

5 The Russian text makes it much clearer that this is a Comintern instruction to the British Communist party to make use of the left-wing group of the Labour Party.

6 A phrase unrecognisable as native English.

7 Lord Curzon was Foreign Secretary in the previous Conservative Governments of Bonar Law and Baldwin, but was their dominant personality, particularly for foreigners.

Organise a campaign of disclosures [unmasking] of the foreign policy of MacDonald.

The IKKI[8] will willingly place at your disposal the wide material in its possession regarding the activities of British [English] imperialism in the Middle and Far East. In the meanwhile, however, strain every nerve in the struggle for the ratification of the treaty, in favour of a continuation of negotiations regarding the regulation of relations between the SSSR and England. A settlement of relations between the two countries will assist the revolutionising of the international and British proletariat no less than a successful rising in any of the working districts of England, as the establishment of close contact between the British and Russian proletariat, the exchange of delegations and workers, etc. will make it possible for us to extend and develop the propaganda of ideas of Leninism in England and the Colonies. Armed warfare must be preceded by a struggle against the inclinations to compromise which are [firmly] embedded among the majority

8 The Executive Committee of the Communist International.

of British workmen, [a struggle] against the ideas of evolution and peaceful extermination of capitalism. Only then will it be possible to count upon complete success of an armed insurrection. In Ireland and the Colonies the case is different; there, there is a national question, and this represents too great a factor for success for us to waste time on a prolonged preparation of the working class.

But even in England, as in other countries where the workers are [the working class is] politically developed, events themselves may [can] more rapidly revolutionise the working masses [the working mass] than propaganda. For instance, a strike movement, repressions by the Government, etc [Government, war, etc].

From your last report [account] it is evident that agitation-propaganda work in the Army is weak [is weakly applied in the Army], in the Navy a very little better. Your explanation that the quality of the members attracted justifies the quantity is right in principle, nevertheless it would be desirable to have cells in all the units of the troops, particularly[9] among those quartered in the large centres of the country, and also among [workers at] factories working on munitions [military needs] and at military store depots. We request that [you pay] the most particular [serious] attention be paid to these latter.

In the event of danger of war, with the aid of the latter and in contact with the transport workers, it is possible to paralyse all the military preparations of the bourgeoisie and to make a start in turning an imperialist war into a class war. Now more than ever we should be on our guard. Attempts at intervention in China show that world imperialism is still in full vigour and is once more making endeavours to restore its shaken position and cause [provoke] a new war, which as its final objective is to bring about the break-up [general outcome is bound to lead to the break-up] of the Russian proletariat and the suppression of the budding world [social] revolution, and further would lead to the enslavement of the colonial

9 One letter is omitted from the Russian word meaning 'particularly'.

peoples. 'Danger of War', 'The Bourgeoisie seeks War; Capital fresh Markets'[10] – these [here] are the slogans which you must familiarise the masses with [spread among the masses], with which you must go to work into the mass of the proletariat. These slogans will open to you the doors of comprehension of the masses, will help you capture them and march under the banner of Communism.

The Military Section of the British Communist Party, so far as we are aware, further suffers from a lack of specialists, the future directors of the British Red Army.[11]

It is time you thought of forming such a group, which, together with the leaders,[12] might be, in the event of an outbreak of active strife, the brain of the military organisation of the Party.

Go attentively through the lists of military

10 i.e. capital (seeks) markets.

11 'Specialists' was the term used to denote former Tsarist officers who were used by Trotsky, some willingly, some under force majeure, to take leading positions in the Soviet Red Army in the Civil War.

12 Apparently referring to the leaders of the Communist Party.

'cells', detailing [choose] from them the more [most] energetic and capable men, turn attention to the more [most] talented military specialists who have for one reason or another, left the Service and hold socialist views [convictions]. Attract them into the ranks of the Communist Party if they desire honestly to serve the proletariat and desire in the future to direct not the blind mechanical forces in the service of the bourgeoisie [not to lead, in a mechanical way, the senseless[13] force which finds itself at the service of the bourgeoisie], but a national army [people's army].

Form a directing operative head of the Military Section.[14]

Do not put this off to a future moment, which may be pregnant with events and catch you unprepared.

---

13 One letter is incorrect in the Russian word meaning 'senseless'.

14 Trotsky played this role when the Bolsheviks seized power in October/November 1917.

Desiring you all success [we wish you suc-
cess], both in organisation and in your struggle
[the struggle],
    With Communist Greetings,
    President of the Praesidium of the IKKI,
                    [G][15]Zinoviev
    Member of the Presidium
    McManus
    Secretary, Kuusinen

15 i.e Grigory.

4
Historical Background, 1924

O N THE TWENTY-FIRST of January 1924 Lenin died. By a coincidence, the Conservative government in Westminster collapsed on the same day when Stanley Baldwin lost a vote in the House of Commons. The King, thinking it only fair to give Labour a chance to govern, invited Ramsay MacDonald, as leader of the second largest Party, to form the first Labour government, rather than dissolving Parliament for a General Election.

This marked the end of the years when government passed to and fro between the

Conservatives and the Liberals. Only eighty five years later, in the form of Liberal Democrats, would the latter return to government, when they were part of the Coalition from 2010 to 2015.

Mr MacDonald's government lasted only ten months. It ended in unhappy circumstances. One of its acts had been to grant diplomatic recognition to the Soviet Union, and so establish formal relations with the Bolshevik regime. Over the next few years twenty other countries would follow that example.

Meanwhile, in Moscow, a vicious power struggle was raging, to be resolved finally in 1929 in Stalin's favour. In 1924 among Stalin's rivals, and thought to be more likely to succeed to Lenin's authority, were Trotsky, Bukharin, Kamenev – and Zinoviev.

And it is with Zinoviev that the defeat of the Labour government at the polls in November 1924 is for ever linked.

After Lenin's death the Soviet government continued to follow the two parallel tracks of foreign policy laid down by him and Trotsky.

They actively exploited any opportunity abroad to organise and support armed uprisings in order to extend the area of Communist power. For example, in the autumn of 1923 they had promoted and directed an abortive revolution in Germany. This track of Soviet policy was masterminded and controlled, under the supreme authority of the Politburo, by the Comintern, the Soviet-controlled Third Communist International. Grigory Zinoviev was chairman of the Comintern.

Alongside the Comintern, the Commissar of Foreign Affairs, Chicherin, used conventional diplomatic methods to defend the Bolshevik state. There was a constant tension between the Comintern, the Commissariat of Foreign Affairs, and the Cheka, Lenin's Extraordinary Commission for Countering Counterrevolution and Sabotage (that is, his secret police and foreign intelligence service.) The Cheka was renamed GPU[16] in 1920 and OGPU[17] when the

16 State Political Directorate.
17 Unified State Political Directorate.

USSR was established at the end of December 1922.

As a Party organisation, rather than a government body, the Comintern was headed by a senior member of the Politburo, which was supreme in Soviet affairs. It therefore enjoyed greater authority and power than the two state bodies.

Despite the tensions between the three organisations all departments of the Soviet state regarded 'British imperialism' as their main enemy.[18] Such was Lenin's clear lead, and it survived his death.

In the last days of the British general election campaign the press broke the news of the English text of a letter purporting to be sent from Moscow by Zinoviev to the Communist Party of Great Britain (CPGB). The letter urged members of the CPGB to increase their efforts to gain power by using the Labour Party as an

18 See *The Foreign Policy of the Bolsheviks*, in *Istoriya Rossii dvadsatovo veka*, edited by Andrei Zubov, volume one, 1894-1939, pp.787-92, published in 2011.

unconscious proxy and by recruiting disenchanted military personnel to form the basis of a British 'Red Army'. Zinoviev wrote with contempt of the Labour Party: the Communists had to exploit and manipulate Labour and galvanise the proletariat.

The letter had reached the Foreign Office via the Secret Service. It may well have been leaked from official circles to the *Daily Mail*. Gill Bennett's immense skill and industry have not yet established beyond doubt who it was who passed the letter to the press and the Conservative Party.

It is possible that the copy sent to the *Daily Mail* was entirely separate from the copy received by the Foreign Office, and was in fact a copy of the version received by the Communist Party in London. No one knows.

The Permanent Under-Secretary (P.U.S.) at the Foreign Office, Sir Eyre Crowe, advised the Prime Minister, who was also acting as Foreign Secretary, to protest to the Russians about their interference in Britain's internal political affairs.

Mr MacDonald commented on the P.U.S.'s draft protest but did not sign it off. The P.U.S., feeling confident of Mr MacDonald's mind, as he later said, went ahead with the protest to the Soviet Embassy and released it to the press. This confirmed the letter's existence and attested to the official acceptance of its authenticity as the work of Zinoviev. Like Lenin and Trotsky, Zinoviev had often written and spoken in such terms, encouraging revolutionary activity in European countries. In the storm that followed, Mr MacDonald never impugned the P.U.S.'s motives; he complained only of the use made of the events by his political opponents.[19]

19 Gill Bennett's book and report authoritatively delineate the tortuous events and recriminations that followed and continue to this day. The reader is referred to that clear narrative. It is not necessary to deal with it further here.

5

Zinoviev's Letter

OVER THE YEARS most accounts of the Zinoviev affair have expressed the view that the letter was a forgery. They have disagreed about how much the bad publicity for the Labour Party affected the election's result, the return of a government led by Mr Baldwin.[20]

20 A.J.P. Taylor regarded the letter's authenticity as 'a curious little puzzle, though of no historical importance.' He wrote, 'there are strong arguments against its being genuine' (*History of England, 1900-1945*, pp.225-6.) Christopher Lee asserts that the letter is a forgery (*This Sceptred Isle: the Twentieth Century*, in the chapter on events in 1924, pp.134-40). Nigel West and Oleg Tsarev assert both that the letter is a forgery and that it played 'a decisive role' in the downfall of the first Labour government (*The Crown Jewels: The British Secrets Exposed by the KGB Archives*, 1998. See p.33 of the 1999 edition).

In her report and book Gill Bennett concluded tentatively that the letter was forged by anti-Bolshevik White Russians in Latvia, perhaps with the connivance of some serving or retired British intelligence officers, acting without official approval.

For its part, the Soviet government always maintained that the letter was a forgery, and the post-Soviet Russian authorities have not changed that line since the end of the Soviet Union.

Whatever the truth about the loss of the election, the Zinoviev letter affair poisoned for decades the attitudes of some Labour leaders and supporters towards the intelligence and security services in this country.

What is the truth?

Certainly the Soviet and post-Soviet Russian denials are worthless. It is important to recall that, until they lost power in 1991, the Soviet authorities, including Mr Gorbachev, denied two shameful acts of Soviet behaviour at the time of the Second World War.

The first was the fact that the Red Army had

massacred thousands of Polish officers at Katyn in 1940. Soviet leaders always maintained that it had been the Germans who had later massacred the Polish officers when they had gained control of the territory.

The Soviet Union also always denied that there had been a secret annex to the Molotov-Ribbentrop non-aggression pact of August 1939. It was under its terms that Stalin and Hitler divided Poland and other countries in east Europe between the Soviet Union and Germany.

It was only after the end of the Soviet regime that Russia and the world were told by President Yeltsin that Gorbachev had had the relevant documents among his personal papers in his safe, proving that he had known full well of these Soviet crimes when he denied them.

There is another point that it is difficult for anyone brought up and schooled in Western thinking wholly to grasp or believe. For a Russophile, like this writer, it is also unpleasant to accept. It is to do with the Soviet and post-Soviet Russian governmental approach to morality. The argument goes as follows.

If Zinoviev and the Comintern, controlled by the Politburo, sent the letter to the British Communist Party in 1924, why did the Soviet Union take such a huge risk? It was a sensitive time, when Moscow could have hoped that its dealings with the Labour government would be greatly in the Soviet interest.

Gill Bennett argues that this question is so powerful, and the favourable developments in 1924 in themselves so great, as to render the authenticity of the Zinoviev letter implausible. She makes good points about how well things were going for the Bolshevik government in their relations with Great Britain following diplomatic recognition.

The problem is that they are good points to the British way of thinking, plausible to the Western mind, but not to those with power in the Soviet state. Gill Bennett's argument does not do justice to the Bolshevik mentality.

This fact is that Lenin and his followers truly and sincerely did not believe in morality or law

or diplomacy, without the preface 'revolutionary.' All these good things, valued as such
in the Western scheme of things, they regarded
as just bourgeois constructs to defraud the proletariat. They were bad unless they were 'revolutionary justice', 'revolutionary morality', or
'revolutionary diplomacy', serving Bolshevik
ends, that is Lenin's ends.

It takes a lifetime to come to terms with this
truth. The Bolsheviks really believed that and
acted on it. In dealing with Lenin and the rest,
we are in the world of Callicles in Plato's *Gor-
gias* and Thrasymachus in Plato's *Republic*.

Lenin's basic and diabolically brilliant
question about all political and moral issues
was, 'Who – Whom?'[21] He always asked, 'Who
has power over whom,' in this way revealing

21 'Kto-kovo?' in Russian. The contrast drawn here between
Bolshevik and Western attitudes to truth, morality and pru-
dence was sharpest between 1917 and 1941. To an important
extent the threat felt by the West during the Cold War kept up
its moral standards. Since the collapse of the Soviet Union in
1991, the reduction of that external threat, now much dimin-
ished, has unleashed forces making the standards of political
life in the West much more like those of Soviet and post-Soviet

Continued on next page

his mind in two Russian words. Power was everything.

Recall the situation as it was seen in the Bolshevik Party and in the Comintern *in Moscow* at the time. In late 1923 the Bolsheviks had devoted huge resources to supporting and to planning revolution in Germany. They spent many millions in hard currency and sent to Germany many of their top leaders, including Radek and Pyatakov.

The uprising in Hamburg on the 23rd of October was a flop. It was not followed by revolutionary action across the country as the

21 *Continued from previous page*
Russia. In his book, *I was Stalin's Secretary*, Boris Bazhanov traces this 'betrayal of Western civilisation' to the alliance of Churchill and Roosevelt with Stalin which saved Communism when it was threatened with destruction and enabled it to seize half the world (p.57 of the Russian text of Bazhanov's book, cited in note 23 on p.38, below).

On the 22nd of June 1941 Churchill knew that he was choosing between two devils in offering British support to Stalin within hours of Hitler's attack. It is difficult to believe that, in his heart, he ever shared the naivete about Stalin shown by Roosevelt and his closest advisers in the White House (see my *A Tear in the Curtain*, 2013, pp.60-2). To this extent, Roosevelt's guilt is the greater as it was not forced on him as was Churchill's.

Soviet and German Communists had planned. It petered out, despite the efforts of tens of thousands of German Communists. The mass of the German population did not want to support a Bolshevik revolution at home of the sort that, through its support of Lenin, Imperial Germany had imposed on the Russian Empire in order to destroy it and, they hoped, thereby win the First World War. There were similar revolutionary attempts and failures, with Soviet planning, in Bulgaria, Estonia and Albania in 1923 and the following year.

What was the reaction in Moscow to these failures? Did the Bolshevik leaders pull in their horns and take a rest? After all, Lenin had died. Had he not been the fountainhead, inspiration and driving force of the Party's desire for a worldwide Bolshevik republic? Quite the opposite: the Bolsheviks turned their attention from Germany to Britain and her Empire. Lenin and his comrades always regarded Britain as their chief enemy, both at home in the British Isles and in Asia, where India was their ultimate target.

Lenin knew that the British Empire could not survive the loss of the subcontinent. In September 1920, the Soviet-controlled Congress of the Peoples of the East, held in Baku (which the Bolsheviks had just seized), declared a Holy War on the British Empire. This was for ever an integral part of Soviet foreign policy, with remarkable success.

We have a direct, personal testimony to this new emphasis on revolution in Britain, after the failure in Germany, from the memoirs of the senior Soviet diplomat, Grigory Besedovsky. Besedovsky found himself under threat from his own side and fled from the Soviet Embassy in Paris with his family on the second of October 1929. He wrote his book about these events and his career, entitled *Revelations of a Soviet Diplomat*[22] in two parts, the first dated December 1929, the second March

22 Translated by Matthew Norgate, in an abridged form, from Besedovsky's text entitled *Na Putyakh k Termidory*, and published by Williams and Norgate in 1931. The quotations given here are in my translation from the much longer Russian text, edited by Aleksandr Kolpakidi, published in Moscow, for the first time, in 1997.

1930. At that time everything must have been vivid in his memory. It is an impressive document.

Doubts were expressed before the fall of the Soviet Union about the truth of certain aspects of Besedovsky's book, for example his meetings with Stalin. However, the diary record of meetings held by Stalin in his office became available in the 1990s. It includes Stalin's meeting with Besedovsky and others on the twenty third of October 1927, on the eve of his departure for the Soviet Embassy in Paris.

That Stalin met his minions at times and in places so as to avoid the encounters being recorded officially is beyond doubt. After Lenin, no Bolshevik was more adept at secrecy and conspiracy. What Stalin lacked in comparison with Lenin in guile and subtlety, he made up for in the fear that he inspired in those around him. Boris Bazhanov's book, *I was Stalin's Secretary*,[23] puts that beyond doubt.

---

23 *Ya Byl Sekretaryom Stalina*, Boris Bazhanov, Algoritm, 2014, Moscow.

What Besedovsky writes about the development of the Comintern and Soviet policy for revolution abroad in the 1920s is entirely consistent with other evidence, and expresses the developments clearly and briefly. It is to be recalled that the Soviet Constitution of 1924 refers openly to the 'Worldwide Soviet Republic', the objective of Lenin and his followers, which the West could not credit.[24]

Besedovsky writes as follows of events in Moscow in the summer of 1924:

A change of direction was also planned in the policy of the Comintern. [Discussion of a plan for an 'agrarian direction' through the Balkans and Italy did not stand up to scrutiny that summer]. That plan was pushed into the background by the discovery of a new weak

24 The Constitution was adopted at the Second Congress of the Soviets of the USSR on the 31st of January 1924. At the end of its first section it reads: 'The USSR [founded on the 30th December 1922] serves as a reliable bulwark against world capitalism and as a new, decisive step on the path of uniting the workers of all countries into a Worldwide Socialist Soviet Republic.'

point in the European capitalist system – England.

A detailed analysis was produced of the economic and political position of England. The 'analysts' were in raptures. Unemployment, the coal crisis, the complete backwardness of English post-war industry compared with that in other countries, the rise in the economic self-sufficiency of the Dominions and India, the loss of the monopoly in trade in colonial goods, the loss of the position as the financial centre, and, most important, the growth of the anti-British movement in the colonies and the growth of a revolutionary movement in China threatening India. The Comintern urgently worked out new routes for revolution. To England was assigned the leading role in them.

The basic direction of the attack was planned in the English colonies and in China. The purpose was simple. According to the theory of Communism, the conciliatory attitudes of the English working class are explained exclusively by their high wage rate, which English industrialists are able to pay to workers because of their extra high profits received in the colonies. Revolutionary movement in the colonies was bound to cut off the means of receiving these extra high profits and compel the English industrialist fiercely to reduce wages.

By this same means they were opening up broad paths to making the English working class revolutionary and to growth of the revolutionary movement in England.

They[25] saw the organisational expression of this revolutionary development in the strengthening of the left wing of the English Labour Party and in the trade union movement.

In the Comintern it was reckoned that this left wing was crystallising into a separate party of an intermediary type,[26] which in its turn would become a good nourishing environment for the growth of the English Communist Party [present author's italics].[27]

The failure of the revolution in Germany in October had caused the Politburo to look for

25 i.e. the Comintern analysts.

26 i.e. positioned between the Labour and Communist Parties.

27 Translated from pp.100-1 of the Russian text published in 1997.

scapegoats. Radek, Trotsky and Zinoviev were candidates for others, especially Stalin, to target.[28] It was recalled, Besedovsky tells us, that in October 1917 Zinoviev was a coward. The Russian word used by Besedovsky means that people in top Bolshevik circles taunted Zinoviev with deserving a 'white feather'. Zinoviev had 'disappeared' on the crucial day. The fact that Stalin also went missing at that time did not prevent him from always viciously citing and exploiting against Zinoviev his cowardice and his vote against the immediate seizure of power from the Provisional government of Kerensky. Stalin played this card ruthlessly until Zinoviev's show trial and execution a decade and more later.

All this made it vital that Zinoviev should show himself a man of determined, brave action in the summer of 1924, advancing the

28 Along with Kamenev, from September 1923 Zinoviev was being used in their 'group of three', *troika*, by Stalin to isolate and destroy Trotsky. It must have been clear to both men that Stalin might well before long turn against them (see Bazhanov, *op. cit.*, p.67-8).

cause of international revolution, the future 'Worldwide Soviet Republic' declared in the Constitution.

The Comintern's analysis of the situation in Britain and Zinoviev's personal motive for writing a fiery letter to British Communists favoured his taking decisive, rapid action. Whatever progress was being made in Anglo-Soviet relations by Chicherin's diplomats could count for nothing against those factors.

In his book Besedovsky makes no mention of Zinoviev's letter. He is said to have confirmed its authenticity in an article[29] that he wrote not long afterwards in an émigré newspaper in Paris, adding that it was Zinoviev's letter, although he did not sign it, rather as nowadays a doctor might dictate a letter and his secretary would type and despatch it to save time in pressing circumstances. The circumstances in the summer of 1924 were like that

29 This article has not been available to me. It is described in Gill Bennett's book, pp.147-8.

for Zinoviev and the Comintern. Action was needed immediately.

The lack of a mention of Zinoviev's letter in his book, in fact, adds to the credibility of what Besedovsky wrote about the Comintern's discussion about the political crisis in Britain that summer and how to exploit it. He is reporting what he knew about that debate in the Comintern and Politburo, not inferring its existence and substance from the letter. It is striking that the letter exploits the situation exactly in line with the Comintern's analysis and thesis, as Besedovsky reports it.

Gill Bennett makes no mention of the evidence from Besedovsky's book in hers.

6

New Light on Zinoviev's Letter

TWO OTHER OLD BOOKS, both by Georgy Agabekov, enable me to cast new light on Zinoviev's letter. Again, they are not mentioned in Gill Bennett's book. Together, the two of them unlock the mystery.

For ten years, from 1920 to 1930, Agabekov served in the GPU and OGPU, successors to Lenin's original Cheka, the Bolshevik secret police set up by him in December 1917. Agabekov broke with the Soviet Union at mid-summer 1930, escaped from the Soviet representation in Istanbul, and made his way to France. He was murdered by the OGPU in 1937 or, more likely, 1938.

Agabekov was a reservoir of information about the Soviet Union and Soviet intelligence. He wished to make it available to the West, to enable the democracies to defend themselves against a new threat, of a sort that they could not grasp, so different from theirs were its basis and mentality.

In an article, 'Unknown Agabekov',[30] Boris Volodarsky called him 'the very first Soviet defector to come from the top ranks of the Soviet secret police'. Dr Volodarsky is, by the way, a severe critic of the good faith and integrity of Soviet defectors. He accepts the assessment of another scholar[31] that two fundamental sources for Western Intelligence after their defections, Walter Krivitsky and Alexander Orlov, successfully pretended that their importance in Soviet Intelligence was much greater than it had been.

30 *Intelligence and National Security*, 2013, Vol. 28, No. 6, pp.890-909.

31 Vladislav Krasnov, in *Soviet Defectors: the K.G.B. Wanted List*, 1986. That Volodarsky and Krasnov are right about Krivitsky and Orlov is not assumed here.

Volodarsky shows that Western Intelligence lamentably and inexplicably underrated Agabekov's potential contribution to the understanding of the Soviet Union and Soviet intelligence. This failure of Western Intelligence is likely to be the reason that Agabekov does not feature at all in Gill Bennett's works. As the Foreign Office's official historian she was naturally granted access to all government, intelligence and security records about Zinoviev's letter for her Report of 1999. Those records are inevitably shaped by this serious, sustained and irreparable failure of official judgement about Agabekov in the 1930s. It is a matter of justice, and a pleasure, now to repay the debt to Agabekov in unlocking the mystery of Zinoviev's letter ninety years after he made it possible to do so, had our country paid him adequate attention.

Georgy Agabekov's two books have each been published under more than one title over the years. Between July and August 1930 he produced the first work, now available for the first time in Russia. Its title translates as 'GPU:

Notes of a Chekist'.[32] The book was written quickly from notes collected by Agabekov before his defection, evidently over a fairly long period. It is intended to help those countries targeted by Soviet Intelligence to defend themselves from Soviet intentions and activities. Sadly, there is no English translation of the Russian text of Agabekov's book. The passages quoted here are given in my own translation.

Agabekov's second book is a narrative account of his work in the service of GPU/OGPU.[33] It is designed to reach a wider audience. Thereby, he must have hoped to alert Western electorates and democracies to the threat of slavery that they faced if the Soviet Union succeeded in extending its tyranny

32 *G.P.U. Zapiski Chekista* (G.P.U. Notes of a Chekist) Moscow Tsentpoligraf, 2017. In what follows this text is referred to as Agabekov's 'first book'.

33 My copy is entitled *Sekretnaya Politika Stalina: Ispovyed Rezidenta* (*The Secret Policies of Stalin: the confession of a Resident*), Moscow, Algoritm, 2018. Its original title was *Cheka za Rabotoi* (*The Cheka at Work*). It is referred to here as Agabekov's 'second book'.

beyond its borders. This second book is cast in more general terms, while providing the background to the first. It was written soon after the first and published in 1931.

During his ten years with the organisation, Agabekov served OGPU at home, in Moscow, the Urals and Turkmenistan; and abroad, in the Middle East, notably in Afghanistan and Iran. Much of OGPU's work in general and of Agabekov's in particular was directed against Great Britain and the British Empire, especially India.

Agabekov therefore took a special interest in British sources and intelligence. He records, almost in passing, great Soviet successes in obtaining British secret information from agents and from intercepting correspondence. British information was prized by OGPU for its accuracy and scope. Agents were paid more for obtaining it than for intelligence from other governments.

Again, in passing, Agabekov speaks several times of the Zinoviev letter, and this is the heart of the matter. The following three passages authoritatively presuppose and thereby, I submit, put beyond doubt the authenticity of Zinoviev's letter.

First, in 1925, posted to Afghanistan, he recruited an important agent who reported to him on the links between a pro-British local leader there and the British authorities in India. Agabekov hoped, with his agent's help, to obtain documentary evidence of a compromising agreement between the local leader of an uprising and the British. With the help of the first agent, he recruited the local leader.

Agabekov's hope was that the Soviet Union could then publish the document 'to counterbalance Zinoviev's letter published in London.' Agabekov wrote as follows of this operation:

With the help of Hassan-Bey[34] two agents were recruited, first Fuzail-Maksum and then also Kurshimat.

Kurshimat interested us in that, according to

34 He had already been recruited by Agabekov as an OGPU agent.

our information, when he was leading the uprising in the Fergan district he concluded an agreement with the government of India to provide him with aid. When we recruited him we reckoned to obtain this agreement or another similar document compromising the English[35] in order to use it as a counterbalance to Zinoviev's letter which had been published in London.

We began discussions with Kurshimat, and it was soon revealed that he had no such document.[36]

In his second book, Agabekov adds the following information about the recruitment of Kurshimat:

To receive into our hands such a document [compromising the British] in 1925, after the publication of Zinoviev's letter, had a colossal significance for us. The Soviet government could have made play with this document on public

35 Like many Russians, Agabekov and Besedovsky usually refer to the 'English' and to 'England' to stand for the British and Great Britain.

36 Agabekov, first book, p.73.

opinion in Europe. Therefore I had an instruction from OGPU to make any concessions [to Kurshimat] provided I obtained the document.

Agabekov then records his discussion with Kurshimat, who said that he had indeed conducted discussions with British officials.

'But, did you have a written agreement with them or how was it?' I asked the question of interest to me.

'No, there was no written agreement,' Kurshimat replied ...

'For six whole years after this incident', Agabekov writes,

I penetrated the secrets of English political life. In this time we obtained many secret documents of all sorts of the English diplomatic service, but alas, we never found any compromising documents [to counter Zinoviev's letter].[37]

Agabekov wrote his books in 1930 with a

37 Agabekov, second book, pp. 101-3.

wealth of experience of OGPU, the Soviet Communist party and the Soviet bureaucracy. He makes it clear that OGPU was confident that Zinoviev wrote the letter and that it framed its policy and operations on the basis of its authenticity.

The second relevant passage in Agabekov's first book[38] refers to what he calls the unending sensation in the West arising from the Zinoviev letter and Western discussion about the Soviet control of the Comintern. Soviet control was total but was always denied by the Russians.

This sensation was awkward for OGPU. It put its intelligence operations abroad at risk. In 1927 this factor caused OGPU categorically to forbid its officers posted abroad to have links there with those Comintern officers also posted abroad or with local, foreign Communists and Communist organisations. Agabekov makes it clear that OGPU gave this direction because of Zinoviev's letter.

Bukharin, a more cautious man than Zino-

38 Agabekov, first book, p.23.

viev, had by that date taken over as head of the Comintern. Zinoviev himself had, for the first time in his career, been purged from office by Stalin. Despite Bukharin's greater caution, OGPU feared that some ill fated Comintern action, like Zinoviev's letter in 1924, might compromise its clandestine, intelligence operations and agents if it continued to use Comintern links abroad and local Communists.

OGPU's decision presupposes and was caused by the fact that the Zinoviev letter was genuine. Undoubtedly OGPU believed that it had been revealed by a genuine Communist *in London*[39] in the Communist Party of Great Britain.

It seems possible that the original text of Zinoviev's letter, perhaps the Russian text accompanied by an English version provided by the Comintern in Moscow for the CPGB, was copied by a British Communist or agent in

39 There is no hint in Agabekov's books that OGPU or the Comintern entertained the possibility of a leak in the Soviet Union itself through which the British received a copy of the letter.

the CPGB's headquarters; and that the copy that he or she made was handed to the British authorities, or even to the press, who could not explain this without betraying the dissident Communist or their agent who would have been working in an exceptionally delicate position. That may be why the copy of the original received by British Communists has never been available.[40] But this paragraph is nothing but speculation, and Gill Bennett's exhaustive study of the way in which the English text of the letter was circulated in London does nothing to confirm the idea, although it does not make it impossible.

Further, after the end of the Soviet Union, it became known that the most sensitive dealings between the Communist Party of the Soviet Union and the Communist Party of Great Britain, including the financial subsidy, were known to only a tiny number of British

40 Perhaps a disgusted British Communist became a British agent. It would be good to believe that some good came of this sorry work by the Comintern and Zinoviev.

Communist leaders, perhaps only one at any one time. The person chosen had to be exceptionally devoted to the Soviet cause and happy to deceive his CPGB comrades. Perhaps the British Communist leader in 1924 who received the CPGB's copy of the letter, in English and Russian, destroyed it, but only after an agent of British security, or a Communist who was disgusted by Soviet interference, had copied the English text.

To return to Agabekov's testimony. He writes:

> The sensation aroused in connection with the memorable 'letter of Zinoviev', unending discussion in the European press on the issue of the identity of Soviet power and the Comintern, and the risk of betrayal and provocation among our agents recruited from local Communists caused OGPU, in 1927, to deliver a categorical instruction to its representatives in no circumstances to have links with the representatives of the Comintern and local Party organisations.[41]

41 Agabekov, first book, p.23. The Russian text of the version published in 2017 here includes inverted commas around the Russian words 'letter of Zinoviev'.

The Comintern was obliged to accept the stringent and difficult measures taken by OGPU to dissociate itself from the officers of the Third International because of the damage caused to OGPU's interests by Zinoviev's letter and the unreliability, in the Soviet cause, of British and potentially other foreign Communists.

And at another place Agabekov writes:

> In mid-1927 ... a circular came from Moscow.[42] It categorically ordered the staff of the Embassy and the Consulate not to enter into any relations with local Communist Parties. I had to break off meeting the representatives of the Comintern.[43]

The OGPU veto about using Comintern resources abroad was short-lived. As Agabekov notes, the recruitment of foreign Communists and Communist sympathisers was too useful and productive for Soviet intelligence to be abandoned for long.

42 To Teheran.
43 Agabekov, first book, pp.124-6.

The third set of events recorded by Agabekov which caused him to refer to Zinoviev's letter, so showing it to be authentic, is related in the chapter of his first book about OGPU work in China. Agabekov writes of an unexpected raid by Chinese police, in the spring of 1929, on the Soviet Consulate General in Harbin. The police seized important documents from the Defence Attaché and arrested representatives of the underground Chinese Communist Party who had gathered in the Consulate to discuss revolution in China. Agabekov comments that what troubled OGPU was the arrest of the Chinese Communists, not the seizure of the documents. This was, in his words, 'because after the celebrated Zinoviev letter it proved possible to declare any document a forgery'. Everyone habitually and mistakenly believed Soviet denials.

Agabekov writes:

In the spring of 1929 a telegram came [to OGPU headquarters in Moscow] from Harbin from the OGPU resident, Etingon, with the news that the Chinese police had undertaken a sudden raid on the Soviet consulate-general there and had seized important documents belonging to the Military Attaché and had arrested representatives of the underground Communist Party in Harbin who had gathered in the Soviet consulate to discuss questions relating to the Chinese revolution. The telegram seriously worried the OGPU.

OGPU was not especially disturbed about the documents seized from the Military Attaché since it was possible to declare as *'false'* absolutely every sort of document after Zinoviev's celebrated letter.[44]

It is also of interest that, during his posting in Persia, Agabekov had personal and professional contact with a GPU officer who had served in London in 1924 and so had witnessed the Zinoviev scandal at first hand. This officer, referred to by Agabekov simply as Braun, was an English-speaker and a friend of the head of the foreign department of OGPU. After diplomatic relations with the Soviet Union were

44 Agabekov, first book, pp.165-6.

broken off by Britain, Braun was posted to China and from there to Persia. Braun was a longstanding member of the Soviet Communist Party. Agabekov, with his deep interest in and knowledge of British affairs and intelligence, had ample opportunity to discuss Zinoviev's letter with him.

Agabekov writes of his dealings with Braun as follows:

I did not reach Teheran before telegrams began to arrive from Meshed from the Soviet consul, Krzheminsky, and from the OGPU resident. The consul asked that the resident be withdrawn and the resident demanded the withdrawal of the consul. In view of the great importance of Meshed to us (we were obtaining English correspondence there), I postponed taking over business in Tehran and set off for Meshed, on the pretext of inspecting Soviet economic organisations there.

In Meshed I found the dispute between the consul and Braun, the OGPU resident, at its height. The conflict had flared up because of the wife of Levenson, the consulate's secretary. Both men were infatuated with her, and she gave her preference in turn to the consul and the resident.

Braun was an old member of the Party and a personal friend of Trilisser.[45] In 1924 he had worked for OGPU in London, and then, after diplomatic relations were broken off with England[46] he was sent to China, and from China, because he knew the English language, he was posted to Meshed to deal with the intercepted English official correspondence.

By profession Braun was a jeweller; he could hardly read or write. He was sent abroad in the service of OGPU only because of his friendship with Trilisser and his knowledge of the English language.[47]

At the time of Zinoviev's letter in 1924 and Braun's presence in London, the business of the Comintern and of OGPU was closely connected. Braun was well informed in both Party and OGPU affairs. Agabekov's relations with

45 The head of OGPU's foreign department.
46 In 1927.
47 Agabekov, first book, p.86.

Braun mean that his conviction that Zinoviev wrote the letter is that much more valuable as evidence of the letter's authenticity.

Further, in OGPU headquarters in Moscow, Agabekov also knew Klyucharev who had served in London until some date in 1926 or 1927. Klyucharev was a politically aware person who refused, on his return to Moscow from London, to remain a member of the Communist Party.

Agabekov writes of him:

The financial section of the foreign department of OGPU is completely isolated from OGPU's general financial department. The head of it is Klyucharev, a young man, about thirty years old, in charge of the work for six years. Before that he worked in London together with Rozengolts,[48] but he had a stormy dispute with the Ambas-

---

48 Arkady Rozengolts was Soviet Ambassador in London from 1925 or 1926 to 1927, when diplomatic relations were broken off by Great Britain largely because of Soviet espionage and propaganda activities. Rozengolts is said to have played a leading role in organising this work.

sador, came back to Moscow and no longer wished to be a member of the Party, despite many admonitions from the Party cell. However, Klyucharev enjoys the full confidence of both the Party and OGPU.[49]

Klyucharev seems to have been a man of political principle. It is conceivable that the cause of his disillusion with the Party may have been in some way connected with the Comintern's handling of Zinoviev's letter to the Communist Party of Great Britain or its treatment of foreign Communists as Soviet lackeys, but, sadly, there is no trace of the reason in Agabekov's books.

49 Agabekov, first book, p.27. Writing in 1930, Agabekov has made a mistake about the length of Klyucharev's leadership of the financial section, unless some of the 'six years' preceded the posting to London.

7

Escape From
the OGPU

AGABEKOV ESCAPED from OGPU in April-May 1930 when it had formulated and was about to implement a plan to take him back to Moscow, by force if need be. His escape and journey to France were helped by his contact with an English woman whom he later married and with whom he lived for several years; and by his contact with British Intelligence.[50]

50 See *The Storm Petrels* by Gordon Brooke Shepherd, 1977. The tone of this account of Agabekov's value to western interests, based on partial access to information from British intelligence records, diminishes it in the way described by Volodarsky. Even his looks are denigrated. It suggests that even until the 1970s British intelligence and security officers were blind to what Agabekov had offered them in 1930. The mishandling of the situation then may well explain, in part, why Agabekov went off the rails later, as *The Storm Petrels* describes.

However, there is no evidence that the British Intelligence Service had any role in shaping Agabekov's books or his words about the Zinoviev letter. It seems possible that British intelligence and security officers did not even know in those days of his books, let alone understand their significance, so incompetent were their dealings with him.

Had they known what he wrote about Zinoviev's letter in his two books, surely they and the Conservative-dominated National Government, formed in 1931 to replace the second Labour Government, would have made much of his testimony. What Agabekov recorded, strongly supported the correctness of official actions in October 1924.

Mr MacDonald himself, Prime Minister in the National Government from 1931 to 1935, would have been more than interested to learn the truth about Zinoviev's letter. Had British officials shown a proper interest in and care for Agabekov, they would undoubtedly have obtained much more information about the letter and Comintern actions in 1924 directly from him than what he recorded, almost in passing, in his books.

Apart from anything else, knowledge of the letter's authenticity would have confirmed Mr MacDonald's stated and evidently sincere desire to believe in the integrity of officials in the Foreign Office and the intelligence and security services; above all, in the integrity of Sir Eyre Crowe, the Permanent Under Secretary in 1924, who had died in the following year, whom Mr MacDonald had profoundly trusted.

Agabekov's testimony also vindicated Mr Baldwin's attitude in public to the Zinoviev letter when he succeeded Mr MacDonald as Prime Minister at the end of 1924. Mr Baldwin privately sympathised with Mr MacDonald's predicament, but publicly always expressed his belief in the authenticity of Zinoviev's letter. The two men were respectful to one another.

British officials could have drawn on Agabekov's evidence in order to justify their attitude to Zinoviev's letter. There is no hint whatsoever of such action. Government, official and intelligence circles simply did not know what Agabekov had reported. It is astonishing, a shameful failure on their part.[51]

51 Agabekov's testimony about OGPU and the Soviet Union generally and his work for the West against the USSR were also disparaged by Alexander Barmine in a book, entitled *One Who Survived*, published in the United States in 1945. Barmine defected from the Soviet Embassy in Athens, via France, to America in the summer of 1937. He held responsible posts in U.S. government service for many years. He died of natural causes aged 88 in 1987. Barmine had served in the Red Army from 1919 and as a member of the GRU, Soviet Military Intelligence, in Belgium, and in Greece where he acted as charge d'affaires. On page 195 of the fifth edition of his book, Barmine states that in 1932, when he, Barmine, was serving in Belgium, Agabekov had provided false information to the Belgian police about Soviet involvement in strikes in the mines at Mons. Barmine does not give grounds for his allegation. Moreover, he had a personal motive in writing what he did: Agabekov's information about the strikes, if it was his, caused Barmine problems in obtaining a visa to return to Belgium after a visit to Moscow. Besides, it is sadly the case that a defector may seek to diminish a predecessor's contribution. As for general attitudes in the West to Barmine, one cannot help noticing, from the portrait photograph in his book that he was, in his looks, distinguished and handsome, not a sorry specimen, like Agabekov, as Brooke Shepherd describes him. This matter of personal appearance evidently and deplorably counted somewhat against Agabekov, if one may judge by Brooke Shepherd's comments.

8

Conclusions

THE EVIDENCE recorded here reveals: firstly, that OGPU and Agabekov were fully confident that Zinoviev had written the letter sent to the British Communist Party. Agabekov always refers to it as 'Zinoviev's letter', never as 'the so-called Zinoviev letter';

secondly, that OGPU believed that Zinoviev's letter was revealed by a British Communist or agent to the authorities in London;

thirdly, that the Comintern was obliged to accept the resultant stringent and difficult measures taken by OGPU in 1927 to dissociate itself abroad from the officers of the Third International because of the damage caused to OGPU's interests by Zinoviev's letter and the unreliability, in the Soviet cause, of British Communists; and

fourthly, and most important of all, that the Soviet Union had, despite all these facts, then succeeded in pretending indefinitely that Zinoviev's letter was a forgery.[52] The Soviet Union thereby learned a vital lesson: the appalling fact was that their lies were widely believed in the gullible West.

This naivety and gullibility, which in some people was replaced or augmented by a hidden or treacherous servility to Stalin's cause and the cause of his Soviet successors, became the Soviet Union's most powerful weapon in its seventy five years' history. It disarmed the democracies psychologically and so changed history.

Was the British failure in Agabekov's case solely a matter of innocent inefficiency? Was treachery also at work? No one can tell.

Only rarely does a security or intelligence

52 Post-Soviet Russia does so to this day.

service, East or West, recruit an agent in those parts of its opposite number who knows about the penetration of its own ranks. It has been pointed out that, usually when this does happen, the agent reveals a spy at work in the security or intelligence service.

We know full well that the treachery of, among others, Philby in SIS, and Blunt in MI5, as Soviet agents, gravely damaged British security and interests from the early 1930s, when they were recruited to the Soviet cause by OGPU, until the 1960s when Philby defected to Moscow and Blunt was unmasked.

Philby's own behaviour as a Soviet agent may be curiously relevant to what Agabekov suffered in 1930. In 1945 he displayed a carefully calculated, self-interested sloth in going to Istanbul to interview Konstantin Volkov, an NKGB,[53] formerly OGPU, officer. Volkov was working as a Soviet consular official in Turkey when he offered the British Consul there a list of Stalin's many British agents, including a

53 People's Commissariat of State Security.

clear lead to Philby himself.[54] Having seen the list, Philby arranged through his Soviet controllers in London that Volkov be returned to his death in Moscow and made his way slowly to Istanbul.

Such a fate was what OGPU intended for Agabekov. Perhaps Agabekov himself was *lucky* to be more or less ignored by Western intelligence after 1930. That there were Soviet spies already at work in British intelligence and security by 1930 seems only too plausible in the light of the list that Volkov gave to the British fifteen years later. At least Agabekov, unlike Volkov, managed to live on for eight years in the West, until 1938. We simply do not know

54 The list offered the British authorities, among many other things, leads to nine British Soviet agents, with their NKGB/ OGPU codenames, who were working in the 'British intelligence organs' and the Foreign Office, and a list of documents, with photocopies of some of the documents, passed to Soviet intelligence by these agents. This material might well have enabled the British to identify the agents. Volkov also stated that he knew that one of the NKGB agents was the acting head of a department of the British counter-intelligence directorate in London; this was later judged to be Philby, a point that Philby himself grasped rather more quickly.

if any Soviet spy in the security and intelligence services, which had desultory contact with Agabekov between 1930 and 1938, was working to speed his murder.

The intellectual, social, political and moral environment in British and other Western official, intellectual and journalistic circles in the 1920s and 1930s certainly did much to advance the Soviet cause.

Agabekov records his amazement that the Western press and public believed that the Comintern, headed by Zinoviev, later by Bukharin, was not an arm of Soviet government as much as were Embassies, Consulates and Trade Delegations.

'They do not wish to understand it,' he writes, 'and deliberately they ignore the fact that the head of the Comintern is also a member of the all-powerful Politburo.' He records:

It is surprising how stubborn is the blindness of some state officials in Europe. Until the present day[55] many of them do not wish to

55 Agabekov was writing in 1930.

understand that there never has been, and is not now, any separation between the Soviet state and the Third International. It could not be so in the past, and cannot be so now.

Is it possible that they are not convinced by the fact that the chairman of the Comintern, now called the general secretary, always combines that post with being a member of the Politburo of the Central Committee of the Party; that is, that he is a member of the organisation which in fact controls Soviet policy and directs the Soviet state.

The first chairman of the Comintern, Zinoviev, was simultaneously one of the active leaders of the Politburo. His successor, Bukharin, was not only a member of the Politburo but was at the same time the official ideologue of the Russian Communist Party. And, finally, Molotov, the new leader of the Comintern is not only a member of the Politburo but is also the right hand man of Stalin, dictator of Russia.

Therefore there is nothing surprising in the fact that the diplomatic and trade representatives of the Soviet government fulfil faithfully the instructions of the Comintern and frequently manage the Comintern's propaganda in countries where governments have admitted them because they believe the hypocritical declarations and deceitful promises of Litvinov.[56, 57]

It is difficult not to believe that Agabekov's unsatisfactory dealings with various incompetent or ignorant Western diplomats and intelligence and security service officers, after his arrival in France, added to the strength of his words here, words known from many other sources to be totally true.

56 Maxim Litvinov was the senior representative of the Soviet Union at the League of Nations' preparatory commission for a World Disarmament Conference from 1927 to 1930, and then Commissar of Foreign Affairs from 1930 to 1939.

57 Agabekov, first book, pp.92-3.

9

Lessons

THE STORY of Zinoviev's letter teaches us important lessons: firstly, the Western public and press and Western intellectuals have been and remain gullible in believing Soviet and post-Soviet Russian official statements. The gullibility has been exploited by traitors.

Secondly, Soviet and post-Soviet Russian authorities never change their false story until forced to do so by some unexpected change or unauthorised disclosure from their side. President Yeltsin gave Russia, and us, a few years of at least partial access to the truth between seventy five years of Soviet lies and what has followed his departure.

Thirdly, Soviet and post-Soviet Russian

false statements have for many years exerted a malign influence on our political life. We have been ill served by elements in the press and some academics who have led the British public to believe Soviet lies in general. In the particular case of Zinoviev, this Western naivety, cynicism or prejudice caused many people to disbelieve the sincerity of the initial conviction in British government and official circles in October and November 1924 that Zinoviev had written to British Communists to urge them to exploit, for pro-Soviet and anti-British ends, the growing Labour Party, against the wish of almost all its members.

The post-Soviet Russian authorities evidently continue the deception operation about Zinoviev's letter to this day. That is clear from the CPSU and Comintern documents presented to Gill Bennett and her equally distinguished colleague to consult in Moscow in 1998 as she prepared her Foreign and Commonwealth Office Report.[58] The Russian authorities

58 See pp.14-22 and elsewhere in Gill Bennett's book.

have powerful reasons for continuing to lie. Other scandalous revelations might follow their acceptance of the truth about Zinoviev's letter.

The same caution must be exercised in assessing the three documents quoted by Nigel West and Oleg Tsarev in their important book, *The Crown Jewels: The British Secrets Exposed by the KGB Archives*, published in 1998.[59] None of them amounts to evidence that Agabekov's testimony is other than true.[60]

59 The three documents are to be found on pp.40-3 of the paperback edition of the book, dated 1999.

60 The first two documents are, in turn, OGPU and GRU reports dated 11 and 20 November. The first reports information 'which requires checking' that the letter was fabricated in Riga. The second reports the same. The first states that the letter was posted to an address belonging to the British Communist Party. The second states that it was sent to a 'well known English Communist'. These accounts show that in November 1924 OGPU and the GRU were seeking information about Zinoviev's letter. Agabekov's testimony makes it clear that Zinoviev's letter, as a Comintern instruction to be sent to the CPGB, was a Party initiative and was not declared to the Soviet intelligence services. The failure to do so led to OGPU's insistence on cutting links with Comintern officers abroad and local Communists in 1927.

Continued on next page

It is a tragedy for all of us, and especially for members of the Labour Party, that long-standing political attitudes were shaped by the controversy about Zinoviev's letter. The result has been that some in the Labour Party believed that the Party's unscrupulous enemies were native to this country, rather than malign forces, hostile to Labour, in the Soviet Union. That belief has flared up from time to time and has never been extinguished. The Soviet lies about Zinoviev's letter played a formative part in this malady. In fact, it was the Soviet Union, and those British Communists with an over-riding loyalty to Moscow, who were together

60 *Continued from previous page:*
The third document is more complex. It is the OGPU record, apparently dated 1935, of a long interview with A.F. Gumansky, formerly active as a White Russian who later became an OGPU agent who was executed in Moscow in 1939. In his long account he maintains that Zinoviev's letter was fabricated in Riga by a White Russian, by the name of Pokrovsky, who was a British agent. He states that Pokrovsky told him that he had forged the letter. Pokrovsky moved to South America. Part of Gumansky's account also emerged in a trial in Berlin in 1929. Given the evidence from Agabekov within OGPU, Pokrovsky's claim appears to be an idle boast, designed to increase his apparent importance and standing.

prepared to diminish the Labour Party and to use it as nothing but a tool for their own revolutionary, violent and totalitarian ends which Labour did not share.

Further, the tragedy was wholly unnecessary. By 1930 the little known but brave Georgy Agabekov, in his books, gave all the evidence needed to show that Zinoviev really did write his letter and expressed Soviet and Communist contempt for the British Labour Party.

If someone serving in British diplomatic, intelligence or security circles had read Agabekov's Russian texts, discussed Zinoviev's letter with him, and made his testimony widely known, much bitterness and malignity could have been avoided in this country. These terrible effects all derived from the Communist Party of the Soviet Union and the Comintern. A proper respect between our great political Parties could have been preserved. It has been and remains a national tragedy. Whether some British official, himself a Soviet agent, did in fact read Agabekov's books and keep to himself

Agabekov's revelation of the authenticity of Zinoviev's letter has become the new riddle about these events.